Teach Them to Give

52 Scripturally Referenced Offering Remarks for your
Weekly Worship Service

Stan J. Tharp, D. Min.

Scripture quotations are from the New American Standard Version
of the Bible. The Lochman Foundation, 1960,
1962,1968,1971,1972,1973,1975,1977.

Table of Contents

Introduction

Why this book can help you:

1. **Biblically based** principles and truths
2. Tested in the "**real world**" of ministry
3. Supported by a "**track record**" of fruitfulness
a. Under the author's leadership, the general fund for the Christian Life Center has **grown 21 of the last 23 years.**
b. Total growth is from a budget of $958,828 (when the church went through a crisis-senior pastor change in 1990) to over $5,200,000
c. The **average annual increase was 7.65%**

PLEASE NOTE: This book is one of a "trilogy" written by this author (available on Amazon.com) that go together to contribute to church health in a straightforward, effective way. It is HIGHLY recommended to read all three, and apply the principles together. Those who have done so have experienced VERY encouraging results:

1. *Teach Them to Give*
2. *The Financially Healthy Church*
3. *BIG: A God-Sized Vision for Your Church* (Using Acts 1:8 as a template for your church health and growth)

This Book's Purpose and Usefulness:

Scores of books and periodicals exist to provide the pastor with resources to build a good sermon or lesson. However, few if any are written to assist the minister on a church staff with two of the most important minutes of teaching that he/she does in a week…receiving the church offering.

This book suggests that an "offering appeal" should be a teaching time that is brief, Biblically based, challenging and effective. *Teach Them to Give* seeks to provide a type of "giving curriculum" that will consistently build a church member's understanding of our reasons for giving.

Too often, offering-taking is "assigned" to a lay leader or staff member at the last minute ("How about if you take the offering this morning?). Then we try to frantically search our concordances or memory for a good verse on giving…often in vain. The offering is then taken with half-hearted preparation and diminished effectiveness.

This book provides 52 brief offering remarks. Each includes a scripture reference and an accompanying thought. *It has been tested by our staff and board members for years, and I know it will be useful to you.* You may quote the material word-for-word, or simply use it as a starting point and chapter and verse for your own related thoughts.

Important Note: Since I have been the lead pastor of "CLC" (1990) we have experienced budget growth in 21 of the past 23 years. Even in our 2008/2009 fiscal years, a year heralded as one of the worst since the great depression...our general fund completed the year $500,000 ahead of budget (that is well over a 10 % surplus!).

There are SEVERAL factors that I believe contribute to this. I have taught the principles to groups of pastors, and also written about them in greater detail in my book *The Financially Healthy Church.* (Available through Amazon.com). One of the many reasons for healthy giving is the kind of consistent teaching this book is meant to help you provide.

Another essential characteristic of a financially healthy church is a strong sense of vision that guides the congregation and its leaders. Such vision also motivates healthy, obedient giving. For a step-by-step approach in developing this kind of vision for your church, please check out the book *BIG: A 'God-Sized Vision' for your church.* (Also available from Amazon.com)

<u>BRIEF THEOLOGY OF GIVING:</u>

Teach Them to Give promotes an extensively studied and carefully thought perspective on giving. Each verse and remark will in one way or another, promote the following briefly summarized perspective on giving regarding the following areas:

GIVING, NECESSARY FOR THE CHRISTIAN: Giving, in a variety of ways, is one of the primary desires and purposes of a Christian. Maturity in faith brings with it an ever increasing generosity and desire to give.

STEWARDSHIP, NOT OWNERSHIP: A key responsibility of the Christian life is stewardship. The mature Christian realizes that every aspect of our life is entrusted to us to manage and use for God's glory, not selfish gain.

TITHING, A REFLECTION OF LORDSHIP: Giving 10% of our income (before taxes) to God is a concept begun in the Old Testament before the law was given, and is supported in the New Testament. More than anything else, tithing is an incredibly practical and tangible reflection if whether or not God is really Lord of one's life.

BENEVOLENCE, THE GOSPEL THROUGH GIVING: Putting our "money where our mouth is" is the financial out-working of our faith. Christians must be concerned and doing something about the poor and needy among us.

MISSIONS GIVING, FINANCIAL EVANGELISM: In order to adequately fulfill my portion of the great commission, I must participate in giving to missionary activity, in addition to my personal efforts in evangelism

GIVING AS WORSHIP: Giving is a common and diverse expression of worship to God. There are a variety of sincere motivations from which to give to God.

GIVING AND GOD'S BLESSING: In every aspect of our Christian life, God honors and blesses our obedience and faithfulness to Him. Giving is no exception. God gives back to us in a variety of ways, in the context of a full and content Christian life.

About the Author:

I have been in full-time church-related ministry at two churches since 1979. The first church I served for four years. I have served the second church, Christian Life Center, since 1983 (clcdayton.com). I have been their lead pastor since 1990.

My education has helped grow and equip me for my ministry experiences:

Bachelors: Business Administration, majors in Biblical Studies/Management, Evangel University.

Master of Arts: Pastoral Counseling and Psychology, Ashland Theological Seminary.

Masters of Business Administration: Management, Wright State University.

Doctorate of Ministry: Conflict Management, Trinity Seminary and College of the Bible.

If I can be of any assistance to you, please don't hesitate…direct any inquiries to sjtharp1@gmail.com.

Have a great day!

Stan Tharp

Offering Remarks

THANKFULLY, GOD DOESN'T GIVE US WHAT WE DESERVE

"He has not dealt with us according to our sins, nor rewarded us according to our iniquities. For as high as the heavens are above the earth, so great is His loving-kindness toward those who fear him."

Psalm 103: 10, 11

The Bible makes it clear that God's loving-kindness toward us is far greater than our comprehension of it. Isn't it encouraging knowing that because of His loving-kindness, God does not give us what we deserve? As the Psalmist states: "He has not dealt with us according to our sins, nor rewarded us according to our iniquities."

On the flip side of the same coin, we quickly realize that we couldn't possibly give God what He deserves. If I gave absolutely everything I own, and all I'll ever have and be, it would be no price to pay for God's loving-kindness to me.

Give today, as generously and gratefully as you possibly can' knowing that we could never give God what He truly deserves…and thankfully, He's given us so much more than our iniquities have earned.

WORSHIP HIS MAJESTY...BY GIVING

"Yours, O Lord, is the greatness and the power and the glory and the victory and the majesty. Indeed everything that is in the heavens and the earth; yours is the dominion, O Lord, and you exalt yourself as head over all."

1 Chronicles 29:11

One of the most fantastic offerings in all history is recorded in the twenty-ninth chapter of 1 Chronicles. Here we read of the provisions made for construction of the temple. King David and the entire nation of Israel teach us that an awareness of the majesty and greatness of God is one of man's greatest reasons to give.

David does not complacently say "I've given enough, let the rest of you give to God's work." Instead, we find in verse 3 of this chapter that he gives to God his entire treasure of silver and gold...over and above an already generous offering.

All the people of Israel likewise gave abundantly that day, and the Bible tells us "the people rejoiced because they had offered so willingly, for they made their offering to the Lord with a whole heart..." (Verse 9)

Let's give with the same whole-hearted generosity that has been characteristic of God's people then, and now.

CELEBRATE YOUR FAITH BY GIVING

"You shall thus celebrate it as a feast to the Lord for seven days in the year. It shall be a perpetual statute throughout your generations; you shall celebrate it in the seventh month."

Leviticus 23:41

We celebrate a variety of milestones, special occasions and accomplishments. Among the celebrations in the Old Testament, the people of Israel celebrated completion of the harvest season (Leviticus 23:29) with the feast of booths.

As part of this week long time of feasting and rejoicing, the Israelites gathered daily to give several different types of offerings to the Lord: burnt offerings, grain offerings, gifts, votive and freewill offerings.

Many of us likewise give to God in a variety of ways: we five our tithes, as well as offerings to missions, benevolence projects and numerous worthy ministries. What we find as we search the scripture is that, just like the feast of booths, God's people have always looked at giving as a way to celebrate their relationship with Him. It's time for us to celebrate in this manner today…let's celebrate, and rejoice…let's give!

GIVING TO THE BEST OF YOUR ABILITY

"Every man shall give as he is able, according to the blessing of the Lord your God which He has given you."

Deuteronomy 16:17

In this simple verse we find three important truths about giving. *First*, we find that all of us are expected to give to God. "Every man shall give..." *Second*, we learn that all we have is not our own doing, but a gift from God, a blessing to us. "...according to the blessing of the Lord your God which He has given you..." *Finally*, we learn that God expects us to give the best of our own ability "...shall give as he is able." If it were possible for us to look at our personal financial records today, looking at what God has given us and comparing that to what we give...would you find that you are giving to the best of your ability?

If so, know that your giving brings pleasure to God. If not, commit yourself today to the same standard of excellence in giving that God prescribed in Deuteronomy, chapter 16.

STEWARDSHIP...WHO CONTROLS WHAT?

"While it remained unsold, did it not remain your own? And after it was sold, was it not under your control? Why is it that you have conceived this deed in your heart? You have not lied to men, but to God."

Acts 5:4

In Acts chapter five, the story of Ananias and Saphira can say some pretty sobering things to us about giving. If any story in Scripture can "put the fear of God" in us about giving, it would be the doings and fate of this couple.

Proper understanding of Acts 5:4 tells us that all we have is entrusted to us as stewards. The sin of Ananias and Saphira isn't in that they didn't give the whole sales proceeds to God. It is that they gave begrudgingly, and dishonestly.

God does not dictate to us what we must do with our possessions. He freely gives us them to us and places personal responsibility on us for what choices we make and priorities we pursue with what we have.

Unlike Ananias and Saphira...who gave begrudgingly, demonstrate healthy control over your possessions. Be a faithful steward of what God has given you, as the offering is received today.

19

A MIRACULOUS COMBINATION

"And they said to Him, 'We have here only five loaves and two fish,' And ordering the multitudes to recline on the grass, He took the five loaves and the two fish, and looking up toward heaven He blessed the food, and breaking the loaves He gave them to the disciples, and the disciples gave to the multitudes, And they all ate, and were satisfied. And they picked up what was left over of the broken pieces, twelve full baskets. And there were about five thousand men who ate, aside from women and children.

Matthew 14: 17-21

What happens each week during our offerings is similar to what occurred in Matthew 14: 17-21. There we read of how Christ was moved with compassion for the needs of the multitudes. The disciples gave Jesus what they had. Christ blessed the loaves and fish, and He did the miraculous with it.

Likewise, as we give our money to God, he adds His blessing to it and is able to accomplish eternal dimensions with what we give. Just as in the story of the loaves and fish, our responsibility is to take inventory of what we have, and give all that we possibly can to our Lord. God will combine His blessing with our gifts, and use them, and people will know that Jesus Christ is Lord.

BIBLICAL INVESTMENT ADVICE

"But lay up for yourselves treasures in heaven, where neither moth nor rust destroys, and where thieves do not break in or steal; for where your treasure is, there your heart will be also."

Matthew 6:20-21

Matthew chapter six gives us some of the greatest investment advice of all time. In this passage of the Sermon on the mount, Jesus doesn't warn us against making money, but He does warn us to carefully consider what we're investing it in.

There isn't anything wrong with retirement plans and investment opportunities, unless you yield to the foolish temptation of preoccupation with material gain, without maintaining an even greater passion for giving away much of what you have to the work of the Kingdom of God. If is often rightly said, that a look at our bank accounts, tax returns, investment statements and giving records, would very much indicate where our heart is.

Give today, as your heart tells you to…it's an investment you'll appreciate forever.

CHEER UP...IT'S TIME FOR THE OFFERING!

"Let each one do just as he has purposed in his heart; not grudgingly or under compulsion, for God loves a cheerful giver."

2 Corinthians 9:7

If you're like me, you like to do things in a way that God will be pleased with. That being the case, if we know God likes something a certain way...we try our best to do it.

Well, as it concerns giving, God does have some preferences. This passage tells us that giving is something God wants us to do...in a good mood!

Just as it would be inappropriate to complain to someone about giving them a birthday present, giving isn't something we do grumbling, because we have to do it. Giving is something we should do because we want to do it.

Give, because you've prayerfully decided to do so, and since you are giving...for goodness' sake, cheer up and enjoy doing it, because that's the way God likes to see us give.

As the team come to receive the offering, turn to your neighbor, smile and tell them "cheer up, it's time to give!"

MONETARY IMMORALITY

"No one can serve two masters, for either he will hate the one and love the other, or he will hold to one and despise the other. You cannot serve God and mammon."

Matthew 6:24

Throughout our lives, every day, we're called to choose right from wrong. In our choosing we grow toward Christ, or yield to the immorality of our days. The Bible makes it very clear that such choices between right and wrong are of utmost consequence.

Perhaps Christ posed the dilemma to us best…we cannot serve two masters. Money can also become a substance of economic immorality. "Mammon," the finance that alienates us from our Lord, is money out of the control of God.

In our choice between God and money, we find those people who serve money find it difficult to give it away. We demonstrate that we serve God, by giving our money freely to Him.

PUT YOUR MONEY TO WORK FOR YOU

"No church shared with me in the matter of giving and receiving but you alone; for even in Thessalonica you sent a gift more than once for my needs. Not that I seek the gift itself, but I seek the profit which increases to your account."

Philippians 4:15-17

A common concept in financial planning today is to have your money work for you. Thus, we look for key investments that bring a great return and minimal risk. Some such investments find us as non-working partners in a business venture.

The New Testament invites us to be investing partners in "ministry ventures." All of us as Christians are expected to expend our time and energies for God's Kingdom. However, we are expected to further involve ourselves by giving of our finances to ministry also.

In writing to the Philippians, Paul makes it clear that when we give financially to the work of ministry, we enter into a limited partnership for building God's Kingdom. Not only does God honor those doing the ministry, He also honors those who support it. Make your investment a significant one today, as we become partners in ministering to a world in need.

YOUR PAYCHECK...EARNINGS OR GIFT?

"Otherwise you may say in your heart, my power and the strength of my hand made me this wealth. But you shall remember the Lord you God, for it is He who is giving you the power to make wealth that He may confirm His covenant which He swore to your fathers, as it is this day."

Deuteronomy 8:17, 18

Most of us work hard for a living; and each week...every other week...or on some schedule, we receive payment for what we have earned...or do we? The Bible warns us that this thinking is not totally true, and it can lead us to spiritual ruin.

In Deuteronomy, God reminded His people to remember who He is, and all He had done for them. Such reflection would obviously bring humble gratitude, and the reaffirmation that even what we are able to earn is God's gift to us.

If we fail to realize that our earning potential is God given provision, we could easily be led into personal pride and poor stewardship. It is not my skills, my physical strength or financial clout that enables me to earn. God, the source of all that is good, gives me the ability to attain. Remembering this, makes giving easy indeed!

THE RELATIONSHIP OF STEWARDSHIP

"And God saw all that He had made, and behold, it was very good. And there was evening and there was morning, the sixth day."

Genesis 1:31

The creation story shows us God's intention for the created world we were to live in. Man was in perfect harmony with God, with himself, with others, and with his environment. It is not until man's fall in Genesis 2 that we see each of these relationships broken…distorted.

Mankind is still reeling from the fall, struggling for equilibrium and wholeness. Our stewardship of things is the struggle between us and our environment that began in Eden, recorded in Genesis 2.

TITHING PROCLAIMS LORDSHIP

"Although He was a son, He learned obedience from the things which He suffered. And having been made perfect, He became to all those who obey Him the source of eternal salvation, being designated by God as a high priest according to the order of Melchizedek."

Hebrews 5:8-10

The book of Hebrews concerns itself with explaining the Lordship of Christ and the New Covenant He came to establish. The writer of Hebrews also shows how the Old and New Testaments are consistent in their anticipation and establishment of this New Covenant.

A key point in Hebrews chapters five through eight is that Jesus Christ is Lord. This passage uses the practice of tithing as part of its argument in proof of the deity of Christ. If tithing were simply an obsolete Old Testament concept, it seems the author would not have used it in his efforts to show the lordship of Christ.

The alternative of course, is to realize that before the law, with the law, and after the law in the New Testament age, tithing proclaims Lordship. With this understanding, let's proclaim Jesus Christ as Lord, by the way we give today.

TITHING FOR YOURSELF

"Bring the whole tithe into the storehouse, so that there may be food in My house, and test Me now in this, says the Lord of Hosts, 'If I will not open for you the windows of heaven, and pout out for you a blessing until it overflows.'"

Malachi 3:10

The Old and New Testaments teach us many things about tithing. Did you know that we don't tithe because God needs the money? God has always been able to provide for the needs of His kingdom, regardless of whether or not His people are obedient in giving.

As is true of all God's commandments to us, tithing is a practice that is good for us...we need to tithe! Tithing helps us keep "things" in perspective. (It is hard to be selfish when you automatically give away at least 10 percent of what you earn.) Tithing regularly reminds us that God is the key priority in our life. When we tithe, we experience and learn the joy of giving. Finally, Malachi 3:10 tells us our obedience in tithing gives God the opportunity to bless us in many ways.

We have many good reasons to tithe. There are really no good reasons not to. If you are not yet obedient to God in tithing, begin today...and trust God to bless your obedience; tithing is truly good for you.

28

BLACK AND WHITE OBEDIENCE

"Will a man rob God? Yet you are robbing me! But you say, 'How have we robbed you?' in tithes and offerings. You are cursed with a curse, for you are robbing me, the whole nation of you! Bring the whole tithe into the storehouse..."

Malachi 3:8-10

Proclaiming and living God's Lordship in our lives is an ongoing daily challenge. Occasionally, I've known other people...or even me, who say God is their number one priority...but their (our) choices tell a different story. God, in His infinite wisdom regarding finite man, knew we would need at least one measurement of Lordship spelled out in "black and white." And, since God also knows that He does not truly get "us" until He gets "ours," He established the tithe.

It is reassuring to know that in the sobering process of working out our own salvation with fear and trembling (as Philippians tells us), there is one area of our lives that requires no guesswork...giving! Give 10 percent to God, because it's already His. By doing so, you show that He is Lord, and then...give beyond the tithe to express your love and celebrate God's work in your life.

LESSONS IN GIVING

"...and a poor widow came and put in two small copper coins, which amount to a cent. And calling His disciples to Him, He said to them, 'truly I say to you, this poor widow has put in more than all the contributors to the treasury; for they all put in our of their surplus, but she, our of her poverty, put in all she owned, all she had to live on.'"

Mark 12:41-44

This is one story that teaches us about God's perspective on our giving: First, we see that Jesus took time to notice what people were doing (verse 41). Second, Jesus evaluated each person's actions based on their own personal abilities. He didn't expect the widow to give as much as her wealthy counterparts. Third, Jesus considered the woman an exemplary success because she did the very best she could. She gave an insignificant fraction of what many others gave. But, she was acknowledged because she did her best.

Isn't it nice to know that God isn't comparing all of us at offering time? Our giving is a very personal practice between us and our heavenly Father. Remember as you give: He's observing me, watches for what I will give from what I have, and takes pleasure when I give to the best of my abilities.

IT ALL DEPENDS ON SENDING

"For whoever will call upon the name of the Lord will be saved. How then shall they call upon Him in whom they have not believed? And how shall they believe in Him whom they have not heard? And how shall they hear without a preacher? And how shall they preach unless they are sent? Just as it is written, 'how beautiful are the feet of those who bring glad tidings of good things!'"

Romans 10:13-15

Paul writes to us in Romans about the urgency of reaching all those who need to know about the Gospel of Jesus Christ. The need is as great today, as it was when Paul wrote to the Roman Christians.

We definitely care about the lost, just as the church of the Romans did. Guess what the basic pre-requisite to accomplishing a mission of evangelism is? Indeed, there must be someone who will be the preacher, the missionary, to preach the Word. But the minister spreading the Gospel is not the basic pre-requisite to world evangelism.

In order for us to reach the lost, those of us who don't go do the proclaiming must do the sending; and sending is done by our spending! We "spend" our abilities and our finances wisely, giving generously and consistently because our mission is "world sized."

31

BAD MOTIVE, BUT A GREAT RESULT

"Give and it will be given to you: good measure, pressed down, shaken together, running over, they will pour into your lap. For by your standard of measure it will be measured to you in return."

Luke 6:38

One of the worst ways to live, one of the worst reasons to give, is self-centeredness. Yet, "what's in it for me?" is a common-place attitude.

The Bible repeatedly sounds the theme of unselfishness. To live, we must die. To be first, we must be last. To be served, we must serve. Over and over again we are taught to consider others before ourselves.

Likewise in giving, we are to give generously and unselfishly. Our motive is not to give for me. Such self-centered giving is the worst of motivations.

Interestingly enough, throughout scripture, and in regards to giving, if we practice unselfishness, we ourselves reap a rich reward. Consequently, we don't "give to get"…yet that is the inevitable result.

Those who give unselfishly, prove to God it is safe to bless them. Our giving today does not create some kind of "I-O-U" from God. We simply enable Him to freely give to his children who freely do the same.

BEGGING TO GIVE

"For I testify that according to their ability, and beyond their ability they gave of their own accord, begging us with much entreaty for the favor of participation in the support of the saints…"

2 Corinthians 8:3, 4

I'm sure you would think it would be quite an arrogant way to receive the offering if I got up and said: "If you beg me enough, I may do you a favor and allow you to give in the offering, more than you can afford." Not only would this seem arrogant, I'm sure you'd probably refuse to give, or give only under compulsion.

Yet, did you know that this is an actual description of the way the Macedonian churches gave? This passage tells us that the Macedonians gave on their own accord, beyond what they could afford, and they literally begged Paul for the chance to give.

Such eager giving was motivated by the Macedonians' love for God, and by their desire to be ministers in giving. They wanted to participate by giving financial support to the work of ministry.

Today, as you give, do so with the same zeal of the Macedonians. Know that it binds us in a financial partnership in ministry that is pleasing to the Lord.

NOT TOO POOR, NOT TOO RICH

"Give me neither poverty nor riches, feed me with the food that is my portion, lest I be full and deny you and say 'Who is the Lord?' Or lest I be in want and steal, and profane the name of my God."

Proverbs 30: 8, 9

Most of us would have no trouble identifying that we do not consider ourselves "too rich." More than likely, all of us would like more financial resources than we have. Yet, at the same time, we must honestly admit that we are not "too poor" either.

Indeed, by the world's standards even the poor American is a fortunate citizen of the global society. The wisdom of Proverbs encourages us to find that "in the middle" place…and be comfortably content living there.

If you aren't too rich, and you really aren't too poor, be thankful. Either excess can be difficult to live with and still maintain a proper relationship with God. Giving is a way in which we demonstrate our contentment with what we have.

Because you don't have too much…because you don't have too little…give. Give to Him who blessed you "in the middle."

INCONVENIENT CHARITY

"Jesus asked him, 'Which of these three do you think proved to be a neighbor to the man who fell into the robbers' hands?' And he said, 'the one who showed mercy toward him,' and Jesus said to him, 'go and do the same.'"

Luke 10: 36, 37

The story of the Good Samaritan is often used as a good example of how we are to help others who find themselves in desperate need. From this story we learn the importance of ministering to a person's physical needs, as a means of showing God's love to them.

One glaring contrast between the Good Samaritan situation and our own is the matter of convenience. Inconvenient charity is unheard of today. Even in the church, the offering plate conveniently passes right in front of us each week. Seldom to we really go "out of our way" for charity.

Christians must constantly demonstrate God's love by showing forth their desire to give to the needs of others; whether convenient or not. Today, as you give…think also of other less convenient and perhaps more time consuming opportunities that may be available for you to give.

TIMELY GIVING

"You shall not delay the offering from your harvest and your vintage."

Exodus 22:29

Learning to give, and seeing it as a consistent part of our Christian lives is an exciting challenge. As with any practice that is good for us; exercising, eating right, regular devotions...giving does not necessarily come naturally without some difficulty.

It appears that one of the challenges to giving we experience was also present in the lives of the ancient Israelites...that of timeliness in giving. They were admonished not to put-off their tithing and their offerings. Instead, they were instructed to give in a prompt, regular and timely fashion.\

If you've ever been tempted to pay your tithe and give your offerings "next pay," you've found that it's like putting exercise of until tomorrow...it may not happen. Don't get tripped up and then discouraged in your giving. Give regularly, deliberately, and in a timely and generous fashion.

MOTHS ON YOUR BLAZER

"Do not lay up for yourselves treasures upon earth, where moth and rust destroy, and where thieves break in and steal. But lay up for yourselves treasures in heaven, where neither moth nor rust destroys, and where thieves do not break in or steal."

Matthew 6:19-20

Imagine a cool clear night in the country; you're sitting on the back porch of a friend's farm house. You notice what looks like a hundred moths flying around a lamp post in the back yard near the garage. Now imagine the absurdity added to this otherwise realistic scene. Your friend strolls out the back door, carrying your best wool sport coat, or sweater, and he hangs it on the lamp post…turns, and comes back to the porch.

If this were a true scenario…while the moths tried to land all over your wool clothing, you'd frantically try to rescue it before it looks like Swiss cheese! After that, I'm sure you'd want to know exactly why your friend did this!

Just as foolish as combining moths and wool clothing, God considers it folly for us to store up wealth here…rather than investing it where it will bring eternal results. Our giving today is inflation, rust and decay free!

WORKING TO SHARE

"Let him who steals, steal no longer; but rather let him labor, performing with his own hands what is good, in order that he may have something to share with him who has need."

Ephesians 4: 28

This verse can be seen as a caution against living beyond our financial means. This verse reminds us that we work and earn not only for us, but for others. If we are living to the extent of our income…or beyond, to the point that we can't make ends meet, then we obviously won't have anything left to share.

Accept the challenge of Ephesians to live a lifestyle by which you can afford to share with others. The Bible teaches us that the happiest people are those who have learned to give, and who practice the child-like value of "sharing."

SOMETHING FOR NOTHING?

"However, the king said to Aruanah, 'No, but I will surely buy it for a price, for I will not offer burnt offerings to the Lord my God which cost me nothing.'"

2 Samuel 24:24

Our generation seems constantly in search of getting something for nothing. As a result, we'll play clearing house sweepstakes, fill out entry blanks, collect game tokens at fast food restaurants, all in hopes of the prize.

It's fine to play those games, as long as you don't eat fast food three times a day during their promotional contests! However, be sure that "something for nothing" is not an attitude you carry over into the church.

Christianity is a constant call to committed giving. We are called to give sacrificially to God on a regular basis. We can't offer to God that which costs us nothing. We must give Him our best. But then, that's what He did for us long ago and still does today.

BEYOND OUR IMAGINATION

"Now to Him who is able to do exceeding abundantly beyond all that we ask or think, according to the power that works within us..."

Ephesians 3:20

God has always been able to do that which is humanly impossible. When you think about it, we are witness and participants of a miraculous event every time we receive an offering. It is at this time that we take something as mundane and material as currency...whether that is paper with ink on it, or currency on-line in "cyber-space," and accomplish eternal results with it.

It is humanly impossible to spend money in any way and redeem the souls and lives of mankind. To accomplish this by a mere transaction is beyond all we could ask or think.

Yet, when we give to God, He transforms financial resources into ministry activity, and ministry activity transforms broken lives and yields eternal souls for the kingdom of God. Our response in giving is the beginning of a miracle that can last forever!

WHAT BANK DO YOU USE?

"Do not lay up for yourselves treasures on earth, where moth and rust destroy, and where thieves break in and steal."

Matthew 6:19

Most of us have worked hard this week to earn a living. Imagine taking your money to the bank. Would you trust your money to "Fred's Bank on Wheels" that operates out of a pick-up truck? Or would you laugh at the idea and promptly turn in to the established, well known bank at the same corner?

The answer is obvious. We want to put our money where it is safe and reasonably secure.

From an eternal perspective, no bank or investment firm can promise you the type of safety that really counts. Investments in God's kingdom never depreciate, and remain for eternity.

YOU CAN'T TAKE IT WITH YOU, BUT...

"...And Jesus told them a parable, saying, 'The land of a certain rich man was very productive...But God said to him, 'You fool! This very night your soul is required of you; and now who will own what you have prepared? So is the man who lays up treasure for himself, and is not rich toward God.'"

Luke 12: 16-21

It has often been said "You can't take it with you." Many a minister has reminded us that you never see a hearse pulling a 'U-Haul' trailer. This is the implication of the parable of the folly of the rich landowner...he tried to store up wealth as though it were his forever.

We may not be able to take our wealth with us, but we can send it on ahead of us. Jesus tells us that we can be "rich toward God" by giving our money for ministry. By doing so, we will someday leave behind what we've accumulated, but we'll also find in heaven that our gifts to God helped build His kingdom, and our eternal home.

GIVING IS BETTER

"In everything I showed you that by working hard in this manner you must help the weak and remember the words of the Lord Jesus, that He Himself said, 'It is more blessed to give to receive.'"

Acts 20:35

One of the most often quoted verses on giving are the statement of Jesus "it is more blessed to give than to receive." It's interesting to note that this quote doesn't appear in any of the Gospels; it is a reference to Christ's words by Paul in the Book of Acts.

This simple statement in Acts does indeed summarize Christ's attitude toward giving and receiving found in Matthew, Mark, Luke and John. Giving is a much greater source of joy and contentment than getting. Remember that, as you have the opportunity to give today.

THE RELATIONSHIP OF GIVING AND GETTING

"Now this I say, he who sows sparingly shall also reap sparingly; and he who sows bountifully shall also reap bountifully."

2 Corinthians 9:6

Throughout scripture the principle of sowing and reaping abounds. It is clear to us that people who receive, are also people who give.

Those who receive without giving, or give only what they absolutely gave to, are those who really don't understand a Biblical pattern for giving.

Christians learn to pay attention to their giving and let God keep track of their receiving. Don't worry about giving too much. This can hardly be a problem when God has promised bountiful reaping to bountiful sowers.

SAY IT BY GIVING

"Therefore, openly before the churches show them proof of your love and of our reason for boasting about you."

2 Corinthians 8:24

Advertisers tell us that we can show our love for someone with flowers, diamonds or other sentimental gifts. The Bible would agree that we show our love by how we give.

Paul challenged the Corinthian church to give to the work of the ministry, thus demonstrating proof of their love for Christ. Each week we have indisputable proof that this church is full of people who love the Lord. Demonstrate again today, one aspect of your love for Him by giving.

GIVE HONOR

"Honor the Lord from our wealth, and from the first of all your produce; so your barns will be filled with plenty and your vats will overflow with new wine."

Proverbs 3: 9, 10

Webster tells us that the act of honoring someone is to regard or treat someone with merited respect; and giving recognition to someone of superior standing.

One way that we respect and recognize the incomparably superior position of God…His Lordship over all creation, is by giving to Him. Our priority of gathering together in church, the songs we sing, the prayers we pray, and the gifts we contribute in the offering are all indispensable ways of honoring God. As we receive the offering, honor the Lord today from your wealth, as Proverbs challenges us to do.

EASY OFFERINGS

"Then the leaders of Israel, the heads of their father's households, made an offering. They were the leaders of the tribes; they were the ones who were over the numbered men."

Numbers 6:2

When the Israelites dedicated the newly completed tabernacle, Moses directed all the leaders of the tribes of Israel to give a special offering. The offering given by each of the leaders is quite a laundry list of gifts: a large silver dish and bowl (both full of fine flour and oil), one gold pan (full of incense), one bull, one ram, one male lamb, one male goat, two oxen, five more rams, five more goats, five more male lambs (all one year old).

Such detailed offerings were not unusual for the children of ancient Israel. It almost seems too easy for us to simply get out our checkbooks, or go online, and give. Times and methods of giving have changed…it's a lot easier for us to give offerings today, but the fact remains, God's people still give.

PAUL'S ADVICE TO AMERICANS

"Instruct those who are rich in this present world not to be conceited or to fix their hope on the uncertainty of riches, but on God, who richly supplies us with all things to enjoy. Instruct them to do good, to be rich in good works, to be generous and ready to share."

1Timothy 6: 17, 18

Taking the world population as a whole, if anyone is rich in this present world, it is today's American. Indeed, even the poorest American is relatively well-to-do compared to the multitudes across the globe.

Paul's advice in 1Timothy fits each of us directly. All of us know the here today, gone tomorrow potential of wealth. Our hope and trust must be fixed in God, and our goal should be to practice increasing generosity and a readiness to share with those in need.

Such giving builds the kind of financial security that remains for eternity. The rich of this world, must set their sights on, and give their wealth to, the kingdom yet to come.

REMEMBER FIRST LESSONS

"And do not neglect doing good and sharing; for with such sacrifices God is pleased."

Hebrews 13: 16

One of the earliest lessons we learned in life was how we are supposed to share. Back then, we learned to share building blocks, a baby doll or a toy truck.

Some lessons need constant reminding. Today, as adults we're still reminded to share. Just as sharing a toy truck may have pleased our mom or dad, sharing our resources with those in need is an activity that pleases our heavenly father.

There are many in material as well as spiritual need today. Giving to the ministries of our church is an effective way of sharing to help meet such needs.

PROOF IN PRACTICE

"If you love me, you will keep my commandments."

John 14: 15

Jesus does not judge our love for him by our professions or our promises, he judges us by our practices. If we love Him, we will do what He has commanded us to do.

His greatest commandment is found in John 14: 34, 35 in which He commands us to love others as unselfishly as He loves us. Such love is epitomized by a giving spirit and a life of sacrifice.

As the offering plate is passed, validate your profession of faith with your practice of giving.

ABOUT TITHES AND OFFERINGS

"Will a man rob God? Yet you are robbing me! But you say, 'How have we robbed you?' in tithes and offerings. You are cursed with a curse for you are robbing me, the whole nation of you! Bring the whole tithe into the storehouse…and test me now in this.

Malachi 3: 8-10

Perhaps no other verses in scripture tell us more about giving than Malachi 3: 8-10. Here are a few key points to remember, as we prepare to give today:

First, if I don't tithe, I deny my responsibility of stewardship and I begin to think I'm capable of ownership. In reality, 10 percent of what I make is God's from the start.

Second, if you aren't tithing and giving offerings, you can't expect unlimited blessings from God…you can expect His displeasure.

Third, God doesn't want four, six or eight percent, He wants "ten percent plus." (Tithes and offerings)

Finally, tithing and offerings don't create an obligation for God to bless me, but it does give Him the opportunity to bless me in ways I don't deserve.

GOD'S WORLD

"The earth is the Lord's and all it contains..."

Psalm 24:1

The Bible makes it clear to us that the creator of the universe, is also the owner of it. We are quickly overwhelmed at the power, splendor and majesty of God when we consider His creation.

Our response is to realize He has entrusted this world to us. All we have is simply "on loan" to us from God. We are to be faithful stewards of God's creation.

Our personal stewardship involves efficient, obedient and effective use of our time, our abilities, and our finances for God's kingdom. As we give our tithes and offerings faithfully, we demonstrate our faithfulness as financial stewards God can trust.

GIVING COMES EASILY IF...

"Not that I speak form want, for I have learned to be content in whatever circumstance I am."

Philippians 4: 11

Without an eternal perspective on life, many people strive to gain satisfaction through the things and wealth they can accumulate. Christians know that things of this world don't satisfy a person; if they did, wealthy people would be the happiest people on earth...that is obviously not the case.

Christians know that true contentment stems from one's relationship with God. The contentment Paul speaks of is one which is not influenced by outside circumstances. Maintaining this internal state of contentment, regardless of what we possess, makes giving easy. We can give generously, consistently, and never threaten our personal contentment, if we build it based on who we are in God, rather than on what we have.

HERE TODAY, GONE TOMORROW

"The grass withers, the flower fades, but the Word of our God stands forever."

Isaiah 40: 8

We need to remind ourselves of this verse often. It speaks to us of the fleeting nature of the things of this world. When we realize that all our things could be gone in an instant, we're less tempted to love them so.

When we love things less, we can love God more. The security that comes from growing in our love for God makes it easy to loosen our grip on material possessions. Such a grip makes giving easier, we find ourselves in greater pursuit of the Word of God, and less concerned about the things of men.

THINGS AREN'T YOUR LIFE

"And He said to them, 'beware, and be on your guard against every form of greed; for not even when one has abundance does his life consist of his possessions."

Luke 12: 15

If we overemphasize the significance of things, we experience undue financial and material pressure, and we live as though we couldn't be happy without an abundance of things.

If you're feeling financial pressure, or the need to get more than you have, pause for a moment and gain God's perspective. The most important part of our lives is not what we possess. The ability to live a happy Christian life has no correlation to our financial status.

Today's world tells us what we have says something important about who we are. Jesus promised us abundant life, not abundance of things. With things in the right perspective, we can give more appropriately.

THE BEST REASON TO GIVE

"For God so loved the world that He gave His only begotten son, that whoever believes in Him should not perish, but have eternal life."

John 3: 16

The most costly gift of all eternity, purchased our eternal salvation, and was given as a gift to us by God because He loves us. Such indescribable love can only be answered with a grateful heart, and a life given in service and love.

Christians, who truly understand the magnitude of God's love that would prompt such a gift, have little trouble with generosity. They struggle instead to understand believers who cling to their possessions as though they were theirs to keep.

Give today, as someone who has been overwhelmed with the awareness of God's indescribable love for mankind. Give because you love.

FAITHFULNESS REQUIRED

"A faithful man will abound with blessings...."

Proverbs 28: 20

Faithfulness is a quality God longs to see in our lives. Faithfulness means being firm in adherence to observing of duty. To be faithful we must be consistent over time.

Remember this ongoing aspect of faithfulness when you reflect on your giving patterns. The Bible doesn't say a sporadic or inconsistent man will abound with blessings. It says a faithful man will.

If you've taken an on-again-off-again approach to giving, you can't expect much in return. Make giving a regular, devoted and consistent practice in your life...blessings will abound!

Holiday
Remarks

EASTER

"When therefore it was evening, on that day, the first day of the week, and when the doors were shut where the disciples were, for fear of the Jews, Jesus came and stood in their midst, and said to them, 'Peace be with you.'"

John 20: 19

The first Easter gives us a record of the costliest gift ever given…the peace that is available only through Jesus Christ. This peace was purchased for us with His life, death and resurrection. No other peace throughout history could compare to this one. This peace is eternal, given and living in the hearts of those who would believe.

This Easter reminds us of this incomparable gift. Just as then, Christ offers peace to all who follow Him today. Let's celebrate the peace He has given us, by giving back to Him our tithes and offerings as a token of our love and gratitude.

CHRISTMAS

"In Him was life, and the life was the light of men. And the light shines in the darkness, and the darkness did not comprehend it."

John 1: 4, 5

Matthew tells us that a great star shone brightly in the heavens on the first Christmas. John explains to us that the greater light, the light of men, was not in the heavens that night, but in the manger.

Then, just as now, men often fail to fully comprehend the light Jesus brought to a darkened world. Those who understand the light...wise men then, Christians today, can't help but be motivated to give gifts to the one who brought light to us all. Let us give today as we celebrate the light of His love this Christmas. Our giving may not make much sense to those still living in darkness; we give that they too might see His light.

FATHER'S DAY

"What man is there among you, when his son shall ask him for a loaf, will give him a stone? Or if he shall ask for a fish, he will not give him a snake, will he? If then, you being evil, know how to give good gifts to your children, how much more shall your Father who is in heaven give what is good to those who ask Him?"

Matthew 7: 9-11

We set aside one day a year to honor fathers with cards that say what they really ought to hear all year. We give them gifts (an uncommon reversal of roles) as expressions of love, gratitude and remembrance.

Hopefully, on this Father's Day you also honor your heavenly Father; in your heart, in your life, and now, in your giving. Jesus told us our heavenly Father is eager to give us good things in our lives. Knowing this, let us reciprocate, and give today as an expression of love and gratitude for all your heavenly Father does for you.

MOTHER'S DAY

"His mother said to the servants, 'whatever He says to you, do it.'"

John 2: 5

Since we're honoring mothers today, let's look at some of the greatest motherly advice given in all history. Mary, the mother of Jesus, gave instructions to servants at a wedding in Cana that resulted in Jesus' first miracle.

Although the context and time has changed, Mary's motherly advice holds true for us as well: "Whatever He says to you, do it." Among other things, Christ has instructed His followers to be givers of themselves and everything they have. Give generously on this Mother's Day as the Lord would have you (or as His mother would suggest).

THANKSGIVING RECIPE

"Now this is the law of the sacrifice of peace offerings which shall be presented to the Lord. If he offers it by way of Thanksgiving, then along with the sacrifice of thanksgiving he shall offer unleavened cakes mixed with oil, and unleavened wafers spread with oil, and cakes of well stirred fine flour mixed with oil."

Leviticus 7: 11, 12

The Old Testament gives some rather elaborate instructions for various ways God's people gave offerings. In Leviticus 7, we have a virtual recipe for a thanksgiving offering.

At Thanksgiving, most of us will enjoy favorite family recipes at meal time. Among the ingredients of this Thanksgiving season, don't forget our need to give an offering to the Lord that expresses gratitude.

The offerings we give today are in dollars and cents, rather than cakes and wafers. Yet our motive for giving needs to be the same as that described in Leviticus…sincere thankfulness for God's goodness and mercy toward us.

MEMORIAL DAY

"And if it is disagreeable in your sight to serve the Lord, choose for yourselves today whom you will serve; whether the gods your fathers served which were beyond the river or the gods of the Amorites in whose land you are living, but as for me and my house, we will serve the Lord."

Joshua 24: 15

On Memorial Day, we pause to remember those who have passed away before us, particularly those who died to defend our freedom. Joshua directed the people in a similar time of remembering shortly before his death.

In chapter 24, Joshua calls the people to reflect back on their history, and all who have done on before them. He notes the heroes of their ancestry, and the unwavering faithfulness and direction of God. His conclusion is a challenge to the nation of Israel to choose to serve the Lord in sincerity and truth.

As we take time today to remember, think also of God's faithfulness and direction in your life. Giving comes easily when we pause to remember.

LABOR DAY

"Whatever you do, do your work heartily, as for the Lord rather than for men; knowing that from the Lord you will receive the reward of the inheritance. It is the Lord Christ whom you serve."

Colossians 3: 23, 24

Labor Day is the one time during the year that we intentionally fix our attention on the workplace. We come from all walks and works of life; yet we have one thing in common: while we might receive our pay from a manufacturer, a service organization, a tech firm, or some sales office or government agency, we really work for God.

When you're on the job, realize you are there to do it for your ultimate employer, Jesus Christ. Working comes easier if we realize we're working for our Lord. So also does thanksgiving. Earlier in the same chapter of Colossians, Paul urges us to do all in the name of Jesus, and to do so with a spirit of giving thanks.

In addition to being thankful for the workplace and those who labor there, let's express our thanks to the one we truly serve by giving to Him from what He has enabled us to earn.

NEW YEAR'S DAY

"Therefore if any man is in Christ, he is a new creature; the old things passed away; behold, new things have come."

2 Corinthians 5: 17

Welcoming the arrival of a New Year reminds us that we serve a God of new beginnings. In Corinthians we're told that life is renewed through Jesus Christ. IN the Psalms we're reminded that God's mercies are "new every morning." Throughout scripture, the Christian life is one of an ongoing fresh new perspective.

As you welcome this year, commit your heart to dedicate all of you to the Lord. Make giving an area which is pleasing to God. If you've not practiced tithing and giving offerings as you know you should, start now and make this year a fresh beginning of obedience in your finances before the Lord.

FOURTH OF JULY

"Freely you have received, freely give."

Matthew 10:8

Jesus was commissioning His disciples into ministry and spoke words to them that speak very clearly to us as we celebrate the Fourth of July…"Freely you have received, freely give."

Although the context of this exhortation deals with the broad work of the Apostles, it also speaks to us. For nowhere in the history of the world has a nation so freely received blessings from God than in the United States of America.

Great blessings are accompanied by great responsibilities. Great receiving must be met with great giving.

To receive without giving is to distort God's plan for our lives. We are channels of God's gifts…not vaults.

Today, as we celebrate our freedom as a nation let us celebrate our spiritual heritage as well. Give today as freely and abundantly as you have received.

Made in the USA
Monee, IL
10 March 2021